ISBN 978-0-260-05182-0
PIBN 11023342

FB &c Ltd, Dalton House, 60 Windsor Avenue, London, SW19 2RR.
Company number 08720141. Registered in England and Wales.

TWENTY-NINTH ANNUAL REPORT

UPON THE

ONTARIO INSTITUTION

FOR THE

EDUCATION OF THE BLIND

BRANTFORD

BEING FOR THE YEAR ENDING 30TH SEPTEMBER,

1900.

PRINTED BY ORDER OF
THE LEGISLATIVE ASSEMBLY OF ONTARIO.

TORONTO:
PRINTED AND PUBLISHED BY L. K. CAMERON.
Printer to the Queen's Most Excellent Majesty.
1900.

WARWICK BROS & RUTTER, PRINTERS.

TORONTO

PARLIAMENT BUILDINGS, TORONTO, November, 1900.

SIR,—I beg to transmit herewith the Twenty-Ninth Annual Report upon the Institution for the Instruction and Education of the Blind, at Brantford, for the year ending 30th September, 1900.

I have the honor to be, Sir,

Your obedient servant,

T. F. CHAMBERLAIN,

Inspector.

THE HONORABLE J. R. STRATTON, M.P.P.,

Provincial Secretary.

PROVINCE OF ONTARIO INSTITUTION FOR THE EDUCATION OF THE BLIND, BRANTFORD.

PARLIAMENT BUILDINGS,
TORONTO, November, 1900.

To His Honour The Honourable SIR OLIVER MOWAT, *Knight Grand Cross of the Most Distinguished Order of Saint Michael and Saint George, Member of the Queen's Privy Council for Canada, and Lieutenant-Governor of the Province of Ontario.*

MAY IT PLEASE YOUR HONOUR:

I have the honour to submit herewith the Twenty-ninth Annual Report upon the Institution for the Education of the Blind, at Brantford, for the year ending 30th September, 1900.

I have the honour to be,
Your Honour's most obedient servant,

J. R. STRATTON,
Provincial Secretary.

THE INSTITUTION

FOR THE

EDUCATION OF THE BLIND.

TWENTY-NINTH ANNUAL REPORT.

In presenting the twenty-ninth annual report of the school for the education of blind children, I do not propose to take up the details of the work and the instruction imparted to the pupils, as the reports of the Principal, Mr. Dymond, and the Literary and Musical Examiners, as well as the Trades' Instructor, give very full particulars of the different departments. I will, therefore, confine my remarks to the general management of the Institution, improvements made, condition of farm and live stock, etc.

There has been about the average attendance of pupils during the year, and their health has, with a few exceptions, been good, as will be seen in the report of the attending physician. Owing to ill-health, the Matron, Miss Dunn, was obliged to tender her resignation of the position, and Miss Nelles has been appointed as Matron in her stead. The music teacher, Mr. Burt, also resigned during the year, and Mr. Humphries has been appointed his successor. The vacancy caused by the death of Dr. Marquis, who was attending physician for many years, has been filled by the appointment of Dr. Sinclair. With one or two minor changes in the working staff, these are all the changes that have taken place during the year.

The usual repairs have been made to the buildings, class-rooms, sidewalks, drainage, etc. The houses of the Principal and Bursar have had new heating furnaces placed in them. A heater for the purpose of keeping food warm during the serving of meals to the pupils has been supplied. A number of new wash-basins have been added to those formerly in use in the wash room, and provision is being made for more water-closet accommodation for the pupils. A renewal of the contract for lighting the premises and increasing the number of lights, has been arranged with the electric light company, with a view to lessening the yearly cost.

New and improved grate-bars have been placed in the boilers for the purpose of lessening the expenditure for fuel.

The farm has produced more than the usual yield during the past year, and the live stock is all in good condition. The farming implements are properly housed and cared for, and all the out-buildings are in a good state of repair.

As to the instruction imparted to the pupils of the Institution, I have no hesitation in saying, from my observation of the methods of teaching, during my official visits, and from the reports of the Examiners, that it is thorough and correct in every particular; the lines followed by the Principal and his staff are in harmony with the best conducted schools for the blind in Canada and the United States, many of which I have visited and carefully examined as to their methods of instruction. Those of the pupils who have taken the course of training either in the musical, the literary, or the industrial department, and have graduated, have obtained situations which enabled them to become self sustaining.

I make the above statement on account of the charges that have been made during the past year by some parties who were pupils in the school (although from their age, and for other reasons, they should not have been admitted), that the methods of teaching, the text books employed, and the general management are defective and improper. Neither of the parties who make the charges (and presume to dictate as to the subjects to be taught and the manner of teaching and management), have had any experience in schools for the blind, other than at Brantford, and their statements are made for the purpose of misleading the public, and, if possible, creating a prejudice against the Institution. I have invariably found the teachers, as well as the other officials, attending to their duties and solicitous for the welfare, comfort and happiness of the pupils.

The attendance of pupils during the past year has been slightly less than during the previous year, and I anticipate a further decrease in the future from the fact that a better knowledge now exists as to the management of children in infancy by their parents, and the medical profession, in order to prevent blindness. The per capita cost during the year has been $259.15 as compared with the previous year when it was $252.22.

The expenditure on maintenance and capital account has been kept well within the appropriations of the Legislature.

The Bursar's department is carefully managed, and the books properly kept. I have to thank the officials for their courteous treatment during my visits, and for their willingness to give me all possible information in regard to matters connected with the institution.

REPORT OF THE PRINCIPAL.

T. F. Chamberlain, Esq., M.D.

Inspector.

Sir.—I have the honor to submit my report for the year ending September 30th 1900.

In former years I have drawn attention to the decrease in the youthful blind population of the Province, and the effect it has necessarily had on the attendance at the Institution. The causes for this are not very difficult to determine. The means of counteracting preventible diseases of the eye are now pretty well understood. The specialist in this department of surgery is to be found in all our cities. The eye infirmary, affording means of ready and inexpensive relief is attached to most of our hospitals. The cases by which blindness might have been arrested by timely precautions in infancy, and those in which prompt recourse to the skilled oculist would have averted actual blindness have probably represented one fourth of the young people under our charge. Such instances naturally become fewer year by year for reasons above given. Then again a less promiscuous immigration has deprived us of not a few pupils who, under other conditions, would have gradually drifted into our hands. Looking back for twelve or fifteen years we miss quite a number of cases of this last-named class. It will also be pleasant to speak later on of the increased facilities offered to some of securing employment of a remunerative character, which fact combined with more systematic arrangements for instruction, favors earlier graduation. It is desired to keep the work of this Institution as nearly as may be practicable within its originally designed limits as a school for the education and industrial training of the youthful blind of Ontario. Hence the discouragement of applications from persons of mature years. Admission to those over twenty-one has, of late, been seldom granted.

Pupil Population.

The date of this report, as more than once observed, makes it impossible to state other than approximately the probable numbers of the pupil population for the session. Those in attendance on the 30th of September, 1899, numbered 120. They rose during the session to 135 and we closed with 130. This year we return 113 with some yet to be heard from and applications present and prospective besides. The average attendance for the past official year was 126. The admissions of pupils to the Institution during the same period amounted to: Males, seventy-seven; females, sixty-seven; total, 144. Of pupils on the roll of last session at its close, 130 in number, 103 have returned to date, fifty-eight males and forty-five females. This leaves fifteen males and twelve females to be accounted for as follows —:

	Male.	Female.	Total.
Graduates:			
Work-shop	1	..	1
Music, literary and industrial classes	0	1	1
Literary classes	1	1	2
Industrial (female)	..	3	3
Advanced:			
Music	2	..	2
Industrial (male)	1	..	1
Literary	1	..	1
Good vision	2	..	2
Mental incapacity	2	..	2
Under treatment	1	..	1
Found employment (partial sight)	2	..	2
Died at home	..	1	1
Impared health	..	3	3
Excluded for cause	1	..	1
Detained at home for various reasons	1	3	4
	15	12	27

The pupils in attendance, 113 in number, are composed as follows:—

	Male.	Female.	Total.
Pupils of last session	58	45	103
Former pupils returned	1	1	2
New pupils	2	6	8
Total			113

The ages of the new admissions are as follows:—

	Male.	Female.	Total.
Eighteen years	1	..	1
Seventeen "	..	1	1
Fourteen "	..	1	1
Twelve "	..	1	1
Nine "	1	1	2
Eight "	..	1	1
Seven "	..	1	1
	2	6	8

It will be observed that all the above are well within the age limits. As opportunities will arise for further reference to some of the graduates and other retiring pup it will not be necessary to make special allusion to them in this place.

Objects of the Institution.

Although some twenty-eight years have elapsed since this institution was opened the full scope of its intentions and operations is even yet only partially understood. Occasionally we are invited to receive, evidently as a permanent inmate, some person more . less advanced in life and in need less of instruction than a home. While we hold our selves bound at all times to tender to such any suggestions that may make their lot the easier, the Institution has no place for them. In Great Britain and in the United States, as well as in several continental countries, industrial homes for the adult blind are established. These are resorted to by those who become blind in after life as well as by graduates from the work-shops of institutions. Such an arrangement enables the inmates to take up industries that it would be difficult or even impossible for them to handle singly and alone.

Workers are paid by the week or by the piece. Some reside in the home, others attend daily at given hours. By the latter arrangement family ties are not interfered with and the blind father is able to become an important contributor to the bread winning capacity of the household. The product of some of these homes is very large and, in addition to government contracts and other extensive orders, travellers are employed to solicit business from merchants generally. There is, consequently, a commercial as well as a philanthropic side to these establishments. They solve the great difficulty that always faces the efforts of the adult blind however apt or industrious the individual may be. I do not think that any one of the homes is actually self-supporting. They have all more or less to be subsidized by grants from the public exchequer or private contributions. But of the good they do there is no question. Has the time not come for some initial steps in this direction in our own fast growing provincial capital? To recur to the point I started from, it is for learners, not for the permanent support of blind workers, this Institution is established. And its original and legitimate purpose is best secured by limiting its pupils to the comparatively youthful blind.

Such designation, it is pleasant to know, gives to those in authority a very wide discretion in the matter of admission. The statute constituting the Institution reads: "Such Institution shall be for the purpose of educating and imparting instruction in some manual art to such blind persons as are born of parents, or are wards of a person *bona fide* resident of and domiciled in the Province of Ontario." In another clause it is provided that no person shall be admitted if over the age of twenty-one years except under special circumstances and conditions. Practically, then, the age limits are between the ages of seven, when education may be supposed to begin, and twenty-one. A well developed child of six years may be admitted, however, and a person over twenty-one need not fear that his application will be refused without careful consideration. But he must be prepared to show special cause for its acceptance in order to be successful. The term "blind person" is liberally interpreted to mean those who, by reason of actual blindness, or of impaired vision, or of danger to existing vision, cannot be educated in a public school, or trained to industry by ordinary methods. So our pupil population is made up of (1) those popularly termed and ordinarily recognized as blind; (2) those of various degrees of vision, from the boy or girl who has a faint perception of objects, to the myopic pupil who is hindered or beaten in the race with others by inability to avail of the black-board; (3) those whose sight may be threatened, and who are advised that, by the rest given to it by the use of blind methods, it may be preserved from deterioration. The more widely the opportunities afforded to all who come within the above definitions are availed of the better it will be for them and those responsible for their welfare. We have many gratifying instances of the benefits a broad interpretation of our duties in the premises has conferred.

LITERARY EDUCATION.

With such slight limitations as their condition makes imperative, our pupils in the literary classes follow the lines of the public school work. It so happens that every one of the literary staff is a native of this Province, has been educated in a public school, has been trained in and has taught in the public schools, and so has a natural acquaintance with, and respect for the public school curriculum. Our text books, supplemented by a good library of standard works of reference are, it is needless to say, those sanctioned by the Ontario Department of Education. While there are practical reasons why, with its various administrative duties and branches of learning and industry, this Institution and its sister at Belleville should be attached to the department having charge of the public institutions, it is never forgotten by those connected with its management that it is really a part of the great educational system of Ontario. And our desire is, that the world-wide reputation of that system may suffer in nothing by our morganatic relations to it. Our examiners have always been eminent as educationists connected with the public schools, and their reports show how far we have come up to the standard they set for us.

We have had little in this department to complain of in the way of criticism. The literary classes are those which most attract the attention of visitors. Of these we have hundreds during the session. Among them are many who have not only cultured minds but who have themselves been or are now engaged in teaching. Their testimony is universally favorable to the work done. In some respects it is admitted that our methods are more effective than those of the public schools, and our apparatus is the admiration of most. On the other hand just criticism is never to be slighted and a long experience has taught me that, in every department of life, it is possible to learn something from even the least friendly of critics. He may accentuate trifles, make mountains out of mole hills, and, by his obviously sinister motives, deprive his animadversions of respect. But the management of an institution is made up of apparent trifles, mole hills may grow in the course of time into mountains, and the unkindly critic may discover what the admiring friend has overlooked. So it is not well to treat with entire indifference the comments of even a prejudiced or partially informed censor. The Institution is open to all during school days and hours. Anyone specially interested in its operations or in the education of the blind generally, will always receive a cordial welcome and be invited to satisfy his desire to the full. It has been a source of regret to me that persons occupying prominent positions in the community have not been more frequent visitors. To one and all the invitation is "Come!" The annual examinations of the literary classes have been conducted since the year 1881 by Dr. Kelly, the Public School Inspector for the County of Brant, and Mr. Wilkinson, M.A., Principal of the City of Brantford Central School. The reports of these gentlemen are both minute and copious and the one now appended is not less interesting than its predecessors. One of our male pupils, who is contemplating a University course, is receiving the necessary assistance in that direction.

A very beautiful globe, a perfect model of the earth, in bronze, and embossed, has lately been added to our geographical apparatus. The raised portions and outlines of the continent, etc., are so sharply defined as to be readily traced by the fingers of the blind students. The globe gives in its natural form, easily realized by the mind, a correct idea of our world and the relations the several portions of land and water bear one to another.

The Music Classes.

The strong and very natural desire of some of our senior male pupils, who had concluded or were about concluding their course of instruction in piano-tuning to become self-dependent, and the openings affording them an opportunity for securing employment, has had the effect of rather weakening for a time the music classes. This, however, is but temporary, nor are we without pupils well qualified to sustain the credit of the Institution. Two of these have already won good positions in connection with the examinations of the Toronto Conservatory of Music, another, who has just graduated, is about entering on a further course of study in (I believe) the Conservatory.

Mr. F. H. Burt, for the past two sessions our resident music teacher, and who has recently received the degree of Bachelor of Music from the University of Toronto, having resigned, has been succeeded by Mr. Ernest A. Humphries, a graduate of the Toronto College of Music. Mr. Humphries is an enthusiast in his profession and has the faculty of imparting enthusiasm to his pupils. Professor Ambrose, our examiner in music, calls attention to the absence of electric motive power in connection with the pipe organ. That is now about to be remedied and, by the introduction of some additional safeguards, the difficulties formerly encountered will, we expect, be wholly overcome. The Professor in his very kind but properly discrimating report, alludes to the exactness which characterizes the work of many of our music pupils and attributes this valuable attribute to our method of teaching. The process is a slow one, but it does much to ensure thoroughness and accuracy. Our pupils, even the younger ones, take very readily to the point-print method of writing, in which all the musical signs are represented. Every piece or exercise is dictated by the teacher and transcribed in the point cipher. It will be seen at once how favorable this method is to a correct reading of the music and precision in the rendering. It is possible for a blind as well as a sighted pupil to slur over his study, but a blind pupil has certainly the least possible excuse for it.

People who take a one-sided view of a question are apt sometimes to enquire whether the results of the musical training of blind youths is commensurate with the time and money expended in their instruction. I have had to admit before now that the results are frequently disappointing. But the same remark applies more or less to the whole question of the education of the blind, and so too does it to the education of the sighted. Looked at for its money value to the community what a large proportion of the teaching in our public schools, themselves perhaps the institution we have most to boast of, finds no appreciable return from those who are its objects. Intellectual dullness, stern necessities, hard poverty, and here and there vicious tendencies minimize educational benefits or cause them to seem to be almost thrown away. And so with the blind. With far more excuse than in the case of the sighted a great deal of our work is marred or wasted by adverse conditions. But, granting that much, for I am no optimist in this particular, I say unhesitatingly that the preponderance of good done by a liberal education of the blind far outweighs any considerations of cost. In their literary as well as musical studies the true joys of life are enlarged and accentuated by the knowledge thus gained. In music especially is this the case. A small proportion only may find employment as music teachers, but there is not one who passes through our music classes who does not become thereby a centre of social pleasure and enjoyment, and, what is not to be overlooked, the possessor of a joy within himself. To piano tuners a music course is almost indispensable. Our curriculum is arranged on the lines of the Toronto College of Music, so that we have an exact standard for graduation.

The Industrial Classes.—Piano Tuning.

At the present time this is the most largely patronized industry for our male pupils. That is due to more than one cause. In the first place, all conditions being favorable, we can offer nothing that promises a better means of livelihood, and there is an attractiveness about the work that has a decided effect on young minds. Then again the prejudice which once barred the tuner-graduate's way to employment has been almost entirely removed. It was a great step in advance when, some eighteen years ago the well-known firm of Messrs. Mason & Risch consented to take one of our graduates into their establishment. I believe the firm have never been without one or more blind tuners since. To-day I am told there are four in their factory. There is hardly a factory in Toronto without our representatives. Others are engaged in the same line elsewhere. And this I am bound to say is largely due to the excellent record of those first accepted. It is very pleasant often to hear of some of these among Toronto's most happy and successful citizens to-day. The general briskness of trade will account also for the present prosperous conditions. In fact the demand for tuners has led to the engagement of some who, by reason of youth and inexperience, not less than partial acquirements, had better have remained a session or two longer in the Institution. The last deficiency it is true is soon overcome by the advantages the factory affords. But the first named objection is too often overlooked both by the young men themselves and those primarily responsible for their welfare. The engagement of a resident tuning instructor has been attended with the advantages expected from it. Pupils who, under the old system could command but two lessons per week, now have the teacher with them at every practice, twice, or it may be three times a day. The practice work is somewhat trying especially to beginners. It can be performed either perfunctorily or otherwise as the pupil may happen to be industrious or negligent. It is needless to observe how good resolutions to be diligent and undisturbed by passing attractions are encouraged and how all are stimulated to greater application by knowing that the instructor is at hand to assist them at any moment. In the repairing branch the advantages are not less apparent both as a means of instruction to the pupils and a considerable saving of expense to the Institution.

The Work Shop.

This department has been very largely maintained in past years by pupils who have been admitted after passing the age limit or who have outgrown that limit while still in attendance. Causes already mentioned and the discouragement of adult applications, have much diminished the number of the class referred to. Reports received from many of our shop graduates show how much they have owed to the instruction received in that department even where, in after years, they have struck out another line for themselves. The path of a blind worker in any direction is beset with difficulties only steady perseverance can overcome. That some should fail is to be expected but such cases are usually to be accounted for by personally disqualifying causes that would impair the success of anyone. I do not mean necessarily moral defects but an inability to grapple with emergencies, or to make the most of opportunities. The want of capital, too, is often a cause of failure and discouragement. If the stock of material is exhausted and the worker has no reserve fund he is stopped at once. During the past year there was an unusual scarcity of willow; heavy exportations fairly cleared the market, and I heard with much regret of several worthy and industrious young men who were thus temporarily idle. I hope in future to be able to make arrangements to meet occasional demands of this kind. The introduction by our instructor of the binder-twine packing cane has supplied a new material especially adapted for the manufacture of strong coarse goods. The supply, however, was not equal to the demand and when the several binder-twine factories shut down, work, in some cases, had to come to a stand-still. In order to broaden our work here and make it more attractive, the instructor has lately designed new patterns for a lighter and ornamental class of goods and is prepared to go further in the same direction when a supply of cane suitable for the purpose has been procured. It is also intended that the net-making industry, hammock, etc., shall be transferred so far as male pupils are concerned, to the work-shop instead of being carried on in the main-building. At this work quite a number of pupils, both male and female, have become adepts. Most of our younger male pupils, too, are qualifying themselves in the art of cane-chair seating. In these various ways I hope to maintain the usefulness of the work-shop as a prominent feature in our efforts to find employment for those who do not show special aptitude in other directions. The report of the Trade Instructor follows.

Report of the Trade Instructor.

To the Principal:

Sir,—I have the honor to submit my report upon the operations of the workshop during the year ending September 30th, 1900.

We cannot in this, as in some past sessions, point to our productions being on exhibition at educational conventions, world's fairs or international exhibitions, nor to a number of graduates having completed their course of instruction and left with outfits of tools, models and material wherewith to begin the battle of life. The past session has rather been marked by special efforts to discover and devise increased means and opportunities, with the necessary appliances, for instructing a number of our pupils who are less actively intelligent and efficient than others in learning to employ their hands to advantage. I hope that some of these may be taught to earn sufficient at least to pay for their food and clothing when they leave the institution. One pupil of this class who, for a considerable time I had regarded as almost beyond instruction, earned $29.00 during the late vacation by making coarse baskets. This young man, like many others before him, has been relieved from enforced idleness, a greater consideration than the money product of his labor. Several others, little more promising, have done equally well.

My attention has also been given to a large class of the younger boys who are not yet entered as workshop pupils, but may have spare time after class hours to learn something that will be useful to them. With this end in view cane-seating has been taught to quite a number. Some of these during vacation earned a little pocket money by re-caning chairs.

A completely new line of models and designs for fancy rattan work, suitable for the younger boys, and possibly some of the female pupils, has been introduced, which I trust will prove more attractive than repairing old chairs and also be more profitable.

At the close of last session the usual vacation supplies of willow or cane were given to eight pupils. Seven of these report having used up their material and sold the baskets made from it. The readiness with which these sales were made has given the pupils confidence of success in the future.

We have at the present time sixteen pupils in the workshop learning willow work, etc. Three of the number will probably graduate at the end of the present session.

There is an excellent spirit existing among the workshop pupils, no discontent or fault-finding but a cheerful disposition and an earnest endeavor to make the best of their opportunities.

(Sgd.) THOMAS TRUSS,
Trade Instructor.

The Sewing, Knitting and Fancy Work Classes.

These classes are being conducted with their usual earnestness and thoroughness. The beautiful and useful products of our female pupils' handiwork always excite the admiration of visitors.

The Cooking Class.

The cooking class made a good record of progress last session. It was inspected by the literary examiners who make favorable mention of it in their report.

Type Writing.

The progress of the pupils in the management of the type-writing machine has been remarkable. There are twenty-two at present under direct instructfon, and all who have passed through the classes, and who remain in the institution, have a definite period assigned to them for daily practice.

Health—Sanitation.

Reporting on the health conditions of the past session they would in general terms be pronounced favorable. Beyond one or two very slight cases of measles nothing of an infectious character presented itself. But of individual cases of a serious nature we had a painful experience. For several weeks four of our female pupils occupied the hospital ward and were objects of unremitting care. Two of these still survive, one with weak lungs, remains permanently at home with her friends ; another it is hoped will outgrow her trouble and ultimately return to the institution. Of the other two, one died rather suddenly, the disease of the brain which was the cause, having at the last developed rapidly. She was a quiet unassuming girl much beloved by her friends here, and her family had our deepest sympathy in their affliction. The other patient was just growing into womanhood, bright, clever and a favorite with all. The fatal character of her malady made recovery, it was early seen, impossible. When some additional strength and the warmer weather made her removal practicable she was carefully taken to her home. About three months after leaving us she died. The loss of young people, so many of whose years are passed in such close relations to us, becomes a personal sorrow. It was so in the cases just referred to. But I should do wrong if I did not acknowledge the kind and generous attitude of the near relatives of those who, on these late occasions and others, have been removed by death. Their consideration and confidence have spared us from feeling an undue sense of responsibility.

It is very satisfactory to know that, so far as can be ascertained, no sickness among the pupils has for many years been generated by lack of attention to sanitation. During the period that has elapsed since the institution was established in 1872, there has been a constant growth of interest in, and improved knowledge of sanitary science. Arrangements that, twenty years ago, would have been deemed ample are now discarded. Apparatus which was then worthy of special notice is old-fashioned and superseded to-day. With this change have come possibilities that did not exist Previously for dealing with the disposal of sewage. That was a long, trying problem with us. It was finally solved by connecting our mains with the new flush system adopted by the City of Brantford whose authorities, for a substantial consideration, undertook the work, including provision for automatic flushing, and the constant oversight of its working. Our slightly elevated position favors the arrangement thus effected. The perfect ventilation of all the branch drains had been previously assured. These improvements have been accompanied from time to time by other extensions and interior arrangements conducive to health and comfort. But it is obligatory on us to keep pace with the times, and to do this some considerable structural additions are necessary. On that point all responsible are agreed, and, in the near future, we shall, I believe in this particular, have accommodation to which none can take exception. The fitting up of a new wash room on the boy's side of the building has proved a great advantage and enabled us to make a desirable separation of seniors and juniors during the performance of the daily ablutions. The enamel painting of every basin and bath takes place annually, and no pains are spared, nor is any cost begrudged in securing the means by which health and cleanliness may be promoted.

But the grand preservative of health and the best disinfectant is an abundant supply of fresh air. And this our beautiful and healthful site assures to us. Our pupils being absent during the three summer months do not enjoy to the full the opportunity for recreation the ample grounds afford. But they have no lack of pleasurable exercise during the nine months of residence. They have free access to the orchards and ornamental portions of the grounds, to every part in fact not under immediate cultivation. And during winter the snow plough and shovel are constantly at work to keep the broad walks clear for promenading. I believe there is no institution for the blind to be found anywhere possessing the wide area accessible to its inmates that our pupils enjoy. And they make a very good use of it. I have known people to utter something like a sneer when the natural beauties of the site are referred to, "What good are these to the blind," they ask. But their one-sided notions would be rebuked if they were to give our pupils the benefit of their ideas. As stated in the earlier part of this report all are not what is popularly understood as blind. Many can see enough to really appreciate beautiful surroundings, although they might struggle hopelessly with the type of an ordinary school book. But those acquainted with them know that, with the loss of sight, even the totally blind have acute perceptions of space, can delight in the songs of the birds, the scent of shrubs and trees, as well as shade and sunshine. The present condition of the grounds owes more to natural growth than to expenditure of money. Very little has been laid out upon them for years past. But money would be well spent if it were necessary to the preservation of their beauty.

Reports of Physician and Oculist.

The reports of Dr. A. J. Sinclair, now our physician, and of Dr. J. A. Marquis, who by reason of his late father's protracted and ultimately fatal illness, was for some time acting physician, go more into detail than I have done with regard to cases demanding special notice. In Dr. Sinclair we have a medical officer of large experience and I hope to receive much assistance from him in all matters affecting the health of the institution. But I cannot avoid bearing my testimony to the valuable services and unwearied attention we received from our younger and talented friend and adviser Dr. J. A. Marquis while acting physician. His qualities of head and heart were severely tested during our trying experience of last spring and no one could have stood the trial better. It was deemed advisable more than once to call in physicians of the highest standing for consultation, and in every instance both the diagnosis and treatment proved to be correct. The late Dr. Duncan Marquis continued to give us the benefit of his large professional knowledge until very near the close of his life. His deep interest in his patients and his readiness to impart the results of his information to others will be long remembered.

A rather full report by our oculist, Dr. Bell, is a feature in this year's budget. Attention is particularly directed to the examiner's allusion to cases of preventive blindness. If legislation, adopted elsewhere is not deemed desirable in this Province, the widest circulation of information regarding preventible measures is certainly a duty. The residence of Dr. Bell in Brantford will afford a ready and desirable means of reference in many cases where the advice of a specialist may be very helpful.

Discipline.

In an institution of this character discipline must be maintained by moral influence rather than by physical punishments or restraints. Except in rare instances severity would not be tolerated by public opinion even if responsible authority cared to inflict it. As a rule the pupils of this institution give little trouble. Occasionally some, with too erratic propensities, have to be brought to time, and then the penalty has to be effective. Regulations affecting discipline have of course to be enforced but I am not aware that any exist here which are not recognized as essential in all similar institutions. They certainly are not recent inventions. And I believe they are to-day more liberally interpreted than they have ever been since the institution started now some twenty-eight years ago. Pupils are allowed free intercourse with their friends in the neighborhood if such exist and many avail themselves freely of the privilege. There is no unnecessary restriction to their having access to the city for any proper purpose. In one respect to an outsider our rules may appear somewhat over strict. I refer to the separation of the male and female pupils except when under the eye of the teachers. Social intercourse between boys and girls is prohibited. I believe the reasons for this are but partially understood. I have good reasons to believe too, that the majority of those most deserving to be consulted in the matter would prefer to leave things as they are. I allude to the fathers and mothers of our pupils. And what I have to say is merely what others similarly situated to myself would say if they were appealed to. I notice that, in the new and most up-to-date institution on this continent, lately erected at Philadelphia, the provisions made for enforcing the rules in this regard are specially stringent. Let me say that, beyond the necessity for a due regard for the preservation of the proprieties of life demanded in every mixed family, it is not the present I am chiefly concerned for. In the Institution our pupils are carefully watched over and they are received and live together on terms of perfect social equality. But the social conditions of their lives elsewhere are widely different. And it is not merely poverty and wealth or comparatively easy circumstances that distinguish one from another. Unknown to themselves pupils dwell for years under the same roof whose individual conditions would make association in after life quite impossible. For that reason if for no other, the avoidance of personal intercourse, still more intimacy is desirable. I suppose nearly every male pupil looks forward to marriage as desirable if he can attain to it; and I shall, I hope, not offend feminine delicacy, if I say, that, without undue eagerness, girls often have their aspirations in the same direction. However this may be, the difficulty of the blind securing sighted partners in life must be apparent to all especially as respects the blind young woman. Hence the minds of both are likely to turn more particularly to those with whom they are most in sympathy and who are similarly situated with themselves. And this, while quite unconscious of the stern realities which they have to confront when life's struggle begins. I do not dwell on the constitutional conditions that make the inter-marriage of the blind in certain cases objectional. That applies to some of the blind only. But the economical reasons appear to me to be of great weight. I have discussed elsewhere the question of the employment of the blind. How many openings have they? The problem of their employment to the extent of securing just the means to live is ever an unsolved one, or only partially solved. And the difficulties besetting a blind man in these efforts are not likely to be lessened by the charge of a blind partner and the further responsibilities matrimony usually implies. That there may be and are exceptions I do not deny. I have heard of one or two happy marriages between the blind. But they have been those of persons of exceptional abilities and capabilities. Marriages between the blind, unless accompanied by some fortifying circumstances, are almost certain to end in misery and mutual regrets. And it is wise to avoid the first step towards their encouragement. On the other hand the marriage of the blind with the sighted may be productive of happy results. With the large population of unmarried sighted women it is perhaps not to be expected that a sighted man should prefer to choose a blind girl for his companion in life. That is a question for men to decide for themselves. But that many of our male blind graduates have been happily married to sighted wives it is pleasant to know. And the more such marriages, deliberately contracted there are, the better. To sum up the whole question blindness wants sight and not blindness to help it. Let the blind person be ever so high spirited, ever so talented, ever so independent, he or she wants something sight alone can supply and this never more than in the struggles of domestic life with its cares, duties and recurring troubles.

Let me conclude this part of my report by saying that it is our aim here so to qualify our young people for holding their own in social intercourse that no desirable avenues to enjoyment and free communion with the cultivated and refined shall be closed to them. And there is many a social gathering that, in the accomplishments of a blind guest, may find itself more than rewarded for its hospitality. The seeing world might do more than it does to make the lives of the educated blind happy.

The Grounds, Farm, &c.

Farming, it is not necessary to say, is not the primary object of our location here. It is rather an economical application of land and space, required for a higher purpose, to providing towards the necessities of the case. And, with the ready supply of the elements of plant life our nearness to a populous city provides, we manage as a rule to secure all the roots, potatoes and vegetables, required for domestic consumption and the needs of the farm stock. I never pretend to treat this as a matter strictly of profit or loss. Premises so extensive as ours must be kept in order, circumstances continually call for the offices of male help. So that the farm by no means bears all the cost for labor the figures would seem to imply. This year we have had a very ample return and nearly every crop has exceeded our anticipations. In some cases we shall have a surplus to dispose of. Farm, orchards, and kitchen garden have all yielded abundantly.

The Pupils' Library.

The reproduction in "point" of a number of works hitherto printed in line type has been welcomed by our pupils, to most of whom the former is the most acceptable. Of such works, and of others newly added to the publisher's list, we have this year received the following:—Stories from the East; Beside the Bonnie Briar Bush; Birds and Bees; Tanglewood Tales; Revolt of the Tartars; Marmion; Hawthorne's Wonder Book; Homer's Iliad; The Princess; Lays of Ancient Rome; Swinton's Speller; Paradise Lost; Richelieu; Old Greek Stories; Childe Harold; Schiller's Poems; The Old Manse; Childhood of the World; L'Allegro; Daffydowndilly; Tales of the White Hills; Story of the Greeks (2 vols.); Montgomery's English History (3 vols.); Robinson Crusoe (2 vols.); Composition and Rhetoric (2 vols.); House of Seven Gables (2 vols.); American Literature (2 vols.); Selections from American Literature (2 vols.); English Literature (2 vols.); Extracts from English Literature (2 vols.); Tale of Two Cities (3 vols.); Last of the Mohicans (3 vols.)

The Circulating Library.

The circulating library has now been in operation long enough to enable an estimate to be formed of its value to the blind of the province and the direction in which it will be most utilized. The demand for books from blind persons who have not hitherto been accustomed to the embossed types has not been very large. Where, however, the library has been availed of by such it has been greatly appreciated and in many instances has given a new stimulus to mental energies that were becoming dormant, and a large measure of brightness to be-clouded lives. But to our former pupils, accustomed to reading in the characters used in the institution work, a regular supply of choice literature has been a boon indeed. The number availing themselves of the privilege the library affords is continually increasing and is likely to become larger year by year. The production by the printing house of both old and new works in the point print cipher is a great advantage to the class of borrowers just referred to.

Acknowledgments.

My acknowledgments are once more due to the clergy and citizens of Brantford generally for their continued kindness and interest in the institution. We do our best as opportunity arises to reciprocate their attentions.

I have the honor to be, Sir,
your obedient servant,
A. H. DYMOND,
Principal.

Brantford, October 12th, 1900.

ONTARIO INSTITUTION FOR THE BLIND.

STATISTICS FOR THE YEAR ENDING 30TH SEPTEMBER, 1900.

I.—Attendance.

——	Male	Female	Total
Attendance for portion of year ending September 30, 1872	20	14	34
" for year ending 30th September, 1873	44	24	68
" " " 1874	66	46	112
" " 1875	89	50	139
" " " 1876	84	64	148
" 1877	76	72	148
" 1878	91	84	175
" 1879	100	100	200
" 1880	5	93	198
" 1881	103	98	201
" 1882	94	73	167
" 1883	88	72	160
" 1884	71	69	140
" 1885	86	74	160
" 1886	93	71	164
" 1887	93	62	155
" 1888	94	62	156
" 1889	99	58	167
" 1890	95	69	164
" 1891	91	67	158
" 1892	85	70	155
" 1893	90	64	154
" 1894	84	66	150
" 1895	82	68	150
" " " 1896	72	69	141
" 1897	76	73	149
" " " 1898	74	73	147
" 1899	77	71	148
" 1900	77	67	144

II.—Age of pupils.

——	No.	——	No.
Seven years	2	Eighteen years	11
Eight "	5	Nineteen "	8
Nine "	8	Twenty "	5
Ten "	5	Twenty-one years	2
Eleven "	4	Twenty-two "	5
Twelve "	8	Twenty-three "	6
Thirteen "	9	Twenty-four "	4
Fourteen "	9	Twenty-five "	1
Fifteen "	9	Over twenty-five years	20
Sixteen "	7		
Seventeen "	16	Total	144

III.—Nationality of parents.

——	No.	——	No.
American	6	German	9
Canadian	69	Scotch	14
Danish	1		
English	31	Total	144
Irish	14		

IV.—Denomination of parents.

——	No.	——	No.
Brethern	1	Evangelical Association	1
Baptist	5	Presbyterian	27
Congregational	1	Roman Catholic	23
Disciples	2	Salvationist	3
Episcopalian	42		
Methodist	39	Total	144

V.—Occupation of parents.

——	No.	——	No.
Accountant	3	Huckster	1
Agents	1	Journalists	2
Baker	1	Laborers	27
Barrister	1	Marble-workers	2
Blacksmiths	1	Machinist	2
Butchers	1	Merchants	5
Carpenters	7	Moulders	2
Cheesemaker	1	Physicians	2
Clergyman	1	Painters	2
Conveyancer	1	Piano-maker	1
Cook	1	Plumber	1
Carriage-builder	1	Railway manager	1
Clerk	1	Sailor	1
Cabinet-maker	1	Soda Water M'f'r.	1
Contractor	1	Stone-masons	1
Explorer	1	Railway employee	2
Farmers	39	Shoemaker	2
Fireman	1	Tailors	1
Fisherman	1	Teacher	1
Foreman	1	Teamsters	5
Gardeners	4	Tinsmith	1
Governments officers	4	Unknown	5
Hostler	1		
Hotel keepers	1	Total	144

VI.—Cities and counties from which pupils were received during the official year ending 30th September, 1900.

County or city.	Male.	Female.	Total.	County or city.	Male.	Female.	Total.
District of Algoma	1	2	3	District of Nipissing	....	3	3
City of Belleville	....	....	....	County of Norfolk	3	1	4
County of Brant	....	2	2	" Northumberland	1	1	2
City of Brantford	2	2	4	" Ontario	1	3	4
County of Bruce	2	3	5	City of Ottawa	3	1	4
" Carleton	....	....	....	County of Oxford	2	3	5
" Dufferin	1	....	1	" Peel	....	....	....
" Dundas	....	....	....	" Perth	....	....	....
" Durham	....	1	1	" Peterborough	1	....	1
" Elgin	2	2	4	" Prince Edward	....	....	....
" Essex	2	6	8	" Prescott	1	....	1
" Frontenac	....	....	....	" Renfrew	1	2	3
" Glengarry	1	....	1	" Russell	1	....	1
" Grenville	....	1	1	City of St. Catharines	....	....	....
" Grey	3	1	4	" St. Thomas	....	1	1
City of Guelph	1	....	1	" Stratford	....	....	....
County of Haldimand	....	1	1	County of Simcoe	5	1	6
" Haliburton	....	....	....	" Stormont	1	....	1
" Halton	....	1	1	City of Toronto	17	8	25
City of Hamilton	2	4	6	County of Victoria	2	....	2
County of Hastings	....	....	....	" Waterloo	1	....	1
" Huron	2	1	3	" Welland	....	....	....
City of Kingston	3	....	3	" Wellington	2	1	3
County of Kent	2	....	2	" Wentworth	....	1	1
" Lambton	1	2	3	" York	....	3	3
" Leeds	2	2	4	*Quebec	2	1	3
" Lanark	1	1	2	North-West Territory	....	....	....
" Lennox	....	....	....	Manitoba	....	....	....
" Lincoln	....	....	....	*British Columbia	1	....	1
City of London	1	....	1				
County of Middlesex	2	5	7				
District of Muskoka	1	....	1	Total	77	67	144

VII.—Cities and counties from which pupils were received from the opening of the Institution till 30th September, 1900.

County or city.	Male.	Female.	Total.	County or city.	Male.	Female.	Total.
District of Algoma	2	3	5	County of Norfolk	9	7	16
City of Belleville	3	1	4	" Northumberland	3	8	11
County of Brant	7	7	14	" Ontario	7	9	16
City of Brantford	13	9	22	City of Ottawa	14	2	16
County of Bruce	8	11	19	County of Oxford	6	7	13
" Carleton	2	1	3	" Peel	1	1	2
" Dufferin	1	1	2	" Perth	2	8	10
" Dundas	3	3	6	" Peterborough	11	3	14
" Durham	3	4	7	" Prince Edward	5	2	7
" Elgin	5	6	11	" Prescott	2	....	2
" Essex	9	18	27	" Renfrew	7	5	12
" Frontenac	5	2	7	" Russell	3	1	4
" Glengarry	8	....	8	City of St. Catharines	2	1	3
" Grenville	2	2	4	" St. Thomas	3	2	5
" Grey	9	11	20	" Stratford	2	....	2
City of Guelph	3	2	5	County of Simcoe	11	10	21
County of Haldimand	4	5	9	" Stormont	5	....	5
" Halton	6	2	8	City of Toronto	50	30	80
City of Hamilton	13	16	29	County of Victoria	7	2	9
County of Hastings	5	4	9	" Waterloo	10	3	13
" Huron	9	10	19	" Welland	6	3	9
City of Kingston	7	4	11	" Wellington	10	8	18
County of Kent	8	4	12	" Wentworth	8	8	16
" Lambton	13	4	17	" York	17	15	32
" Leeds	12	4	16	*Province of Quebec	4	1	5
" Lanark	2	4	6	*Northwest Territory	....	1	1
" Lennox	4	1	5	*United States	1	....	1
" Lincoln	3	3	6	*British Columbia	1	....	1
City of London	10	9	19	*Manitoba	1	....	1
District of Nipissing	1	3	4				
County of Middlesex	9	11	20				
District of Muskoka	3	....	3	Total	400	302	702

* On payment.

VIII.—Cities and counties from which pupils were received who were in residence on 30th September, 1900.

County or city.	Male.	Female.	Total.	County or city.	Male.	Female.	Total.
District of Algoma	....	2	2	District of Muskoka	1	1	2
City of Belleville	....	....	....	" Nipissing	....	3	3
County of Brant	....	2	2	County of Norfolk	4	2	6
City of Brantford	2	2	4	" Northumberland	1	1	2
County of Bruce	2	2	4	" Ontario	1	2	3
" Carleton	....	....	....	City of Ottawa	1	....	1
" Dufferin	1	....	1	County of Oxford	2	3	5
" Dundas	....	....	....	" Peel	....	....	....
" Durham	....	....	....	" Perth	....	....	....
" Elgin	2	1	3	" Peterborough	....	....	....
" Essex	....	4	4	" Prince Edward	....	....	....
" Frontenac	1	....	1	" Prescott	1	....	1
" Glengarry	1	....	1	" Renfrew	1	2	3
" Grenville	....	1	1	" Russell	....	....	....
" Grey	4	1	5	City of St. Catharines	....	....	....
City of Guelph	1	....	1	" St. Thomas	....	....	....
County of Haldimand	....	....	....	" Stratford	....	....	....
" Haliburton	....	....	....	County of Simcoe	3	1	4
" Halton	....	1	1	" Stormont	1	....	1
City of Hamilton	2	4	6	City of Toronto	12	6	18
County of Hastings	....	....	....	County of Victoria	1	....	1
" Huron	1	....	1	" Waterloo	2	....	2
City of Kingston	2	....	2	" Welland	....	....	....
County of Kent	2	....	2	" Wellington	1	1	2
" Lambton	1	2	3	" Wentworth	....	1	1
" Leeds	1	2	3	" York	....	1	1
" Lanark	1	1	2	British Columbia	1	....	1
" Lennox	....	....	....	Quebec	2	1	3
" Lincoln	....	....	....	Manitoba	....	....	....
City of London	....	....	....				
County of Middlesex	2	2	4	Total	61	52	113

REPORT OF SURGEON.

T. F. CHAMBERLAIN, ESQ., M.D.,
Inspector Public Charities of Ontario.

SIR,—My report this year as acting physician to the Institution for the Blind is partial, being from the date of my father's death, which occurred a few days after the opening of the last session, to May 1st, 1900, at which time Dr. A. J. Sinclair assumed charge.

The session, with the exception of a few trying cases, was a healthy one.

Early in the year a female pupil developed appendicitis and caused some anxiety for a few days, but made satisfactory recovery. Another girl pupil, with a family history pointing to tubercular disease, was confined to bed for a number of weeks suffering from tuberculosis. By careful and skilful nursing and by the watchful attention of the officials she gained enough strength to be removed to her home in Eastern Ontario, where she succumed some three months later. The one death during the session was a case of cerebral tumor, the patient died after some weeks of suffering. She had shown symptoms of brain trouble for a considerable time but the acute trouble presented itself early in the present year.

During the year there were the usual cases of influenza, among whom, Miss Dunn, the matron, was by far the most unfortunate, but with her characteristic determination she baffled the disease and made a good though slow recovery.

The single case of small-pox that visited our city last winter made it seem advisable to vaccinate the pupils who had not been regularly innoculated for a number of years. A very large percentage of cases proved susceptible to the virus. My report would be incomplete did I not assure you, sir, of the complete satisfaction as regards care and nursing of the patients who have come under my charge during my term as acting physician. It would be impossible to obtain better attention in any public or private institution.

I have the honor to be, Sir,
Your obedient servant,

October 2nd, 1900. JOHN A. MARQUIS.

REPORT OF THE PHYSICIAN.

T. F. CHAMBERLAIN, ESQ., M.D.,
Inspector Public Charities of Ontario.

SIR,—Owing to a severe illness I did not assume the duties of physician to the Ontario Institution for the Blind until May 1st, the Provincial Secretary having kindly given me ample time to recover and approved of Dr. John A. Marquis meanwhile as acting physician.

I found on my first visit a well assorted quantity of drugs in the dispensary, also surgical instruments suitable for all minor operations. The nearness of the John H. Stratford hospital makes a more elaborate supply unnecessary.

The building was clean, well ventilated and everything was neat and orderly. The nurses were attentive and seem to have the welfare of the pupils at heart.

The health of the staff and the pupils has been excellent. No serious case has occurred since I began my duties. Slight illnesses, mostly of a catarrhal and neuralgic character, prevail. Owing to the watchfulness of the officials and the fidelity of the nurses an outbreak of contagious diseases is very infrequent and easily controlled.

After the holidays I examined all the pupils and found them clean and healthy, with the exception of one or two with a slight skin disease which soon disappeared under proper treatment.

The report of the acting physician is appended.

I have the honor to be, Sir,
Your obedient servant,
A. J. SINCLAIR.

To T. F. CHAMBERLAIN, ESQ, M.D.,

Inspector of Charities, Asylums, etc., for Ontario.

SIR,—We have the honor to submit for your consideration the following report of the results of the examination of the literary classes in the Ontario Institution for the Instruction of the Blind, situated at Brantford, for 1899-1900.

The time of examination covered three days as usual, during which the weather was fine, and the beautiful grounds of the Institution were looking their best after the refreshing rains that had but recently followed the prolonged period of dry weather in May. The corridors and class-rooms were bright and clean, as is customary here.

These are the results:

(a) MISS GILLIN'S CLASSES.

(1) *Arithmetic.*—Class C. Seventeen in class. Limit: Simple rules, weights and measures, easy problems. With the first the class showed a very satisfactory acquaintance. The tables had been carefully and accurately memorized. Many problems based upon the knowledge of them were promptly and correctly solved by the majority of the class

(2) *Grammar.*—Class. Thirteen in class. Limit: Analyses and parsing of sentences of all kinds. Earle's Philology to end of fifth chapter. Many sentences in prose and verse were analyzed and the principal words parsed. A competent knowledge of the history of the English tongue—the changes effected in Anglo-Saxon by the influx of other languages at different times, etc., was manifested by the majority. All except two obtained more than 50 per cent. of the marks.

(3) *Writing.*—Class D. Twenty-two in class. Some recently moved up from the Kindergarten. Limit: Letters, words and short sentences. The work was very satisfactory, the grade being considered.

(4) *English History.* A class of eighteen. Limit: William III to date. This class was as thoroughly examined on the subject as time permitted, and as the marks show, did well. evincing a very satisfactory knowledge of the parts and constitutional changes of the period, and something of its literature. Except in three instances the class was marked high and did credit to its instructor.

(5) *English Literature.* Class of twenty. Limit: History of from Cædmon to reign of George III; Merchant of Venice. Quotations from the latter. The interest manifested in this subject is remarkable, and it never flags. For two hours the class stood without flinching a fire of questions that might have daunted one less instructed and less resolute, and replied to them effectively. Of the play they had a very full and accurate knowledge; they must have been very thoroughly and critically instructed. They had made themselves at home with the principal characters. The finest passages they had at their finger ends, and could recite them with correct expression and good taste.

(6) *Geography.*—Class B. This class was examined in the Geography of South America, the United States, Central America, and the West India Islands. The last two but slightly. They gave a very good account of the principal physical features of the different countries mentioned, and are able to locate the chief rivers and cities. Most of them are quite familiar with the map and quite readily recognize any part when separated from the rest and are able to give the adjoining countries and the chief items of interest in connection with it.

(7) *Canadian History.* The class had studied the period from 1763 to the present. The information is mainly conveyed in oral lessons by the teacher, and hence the work is far more difficult for both teacher and pupils than in the case of those who have the aid of text-books. We found the class had mastered the outlines of the most important events, and had a good general idea of some of the principal men of the period. Perhaps a little more biography could be given without taxing the pupils. The class did better than that of last year, the answering being more uniform. The class marks were 84 per cent.

(8) *Bible Class.*—Girls. The pupils were able to give a very good synopsis of the Acts of the Apostles, following the narrative chapter by chapter. Each pupil commenced

where the examiner desired the previous pupil to stop and so proceeding, being constantly questioned upon the matters mentioned until the whole book was gone through. In pretty much the same way the first six chapters of Genesis were treated. The examination was eminently satisfactory, fifteen pupils not having missed any questions. There were twenty young ladies in the class.

(b) MISS WALSHE'S CLASSES.

(1) Class D. Twenty-three in class. Limit: Ontario—Counties, cities, rivers, lakes, products, railways. With a couple of exceptions the class did remarkably good work. They knew the counties, county towns, principal cities, etc., very thoroughly, and were able to show them by means of the dissected map; could point out the lakes, trace the rivers and give in detail the products of the Province. In a knowledge of the railways they excelled—running with their fingers up and down each line, naming the principal centres of population and facts connected with them. No fewer than twelve got the maximum.

(2) *Reading*.—Class B. Seventeen in class. Reading from five different books. Good articulation, expression and correct emphasis had been well looked after. None obtained less than half marks.

(3) *Writing*.—Class C. Nineteen in class. Limit: Capitals and small letters, figures, lists of words, sentences. The work, as the marks show, was very well done, and the subject had evidently been carefully and conscientiously taught.

(4) *Arithmetic*.—Class A. The class consists of thirteen pupils—eight boys and five girls. Their course comprises measures, multiples, percentage with its applications to profit and loss. Interest and its general use. Partnership, discount and mensuration as applied to rectangles, circles, etc. All these were covered by the questions given. The work was done quickly, and, as may be seen by the percentages obtained, accurately. Eight pupils obtained over 70 per cent. of the marks. The method of teaching the subject by Miss Walshe develops the logical faculty. There is very little of "remembering laws," but an intelligent application of principles. The tone and order of the pupils are perfect. Their desire to do well is very evident.

(5) *Bible Study*. There are sixteen pupils in this class. They were examined on the Gospel of St. Luke. They had very thoroughly mastered the subject, knowing the parables, miracles, the magnificat and indeed all the chief parts of the Gospel. They are very well acquainted with the history of the book, the lives of the chief persons referred to in it, and, in fact, have made a very complete study of the work assigned. The pupils are Roman Catholics and use their version of the Scriptures.

(6) *Grammar*.—B. Very few classes have done better work than this. Their knowledge of technical grammar as far at their course goes, is good. They parse very well, correct errors in English and give intelligent reasons for their connections. They express themselves in good English, and are very accurate, some of them even to preciseness, in their statement of answers. The class has had the foundation of the subject very well laid.

(c) MR. WICKENS' CLASS.

(1) *Reading*.—Class A. Thirteen in class. This is a class of excellent readers with three exceptions. They read prose and verse with fluency, expression, correct emphasis and good taste, showing that they know what they read. They also duly appreciate the literature, the meanings of the words and phrases in the lessons. In spelling also, they showed themselves proficient, being able to spell readily the most difficult words in the text as well as others taken from the "Practical Speller."

(2) *Bible Class*—Boys, A. Twenty present in class. Limit: Apostolic History, Acts. Bible study has recently become a prominent feature of the teaching of the Institution. This class showed by their answers that they had been carefully and rather minutely instructed in the history of the important events that immediately followed the death of our Lord. They were familiar with the principal facts and the leading characters in Acts. The lowest mark was 70 per cent.

(3) *Arithmetic*.—B. There are fifteen pupils in this class. The class is an exceptionally good one. They are very cheerful and earnest in their work, do it in a remark-

ably short time. Eight of them made 80 per cent. or over of the marks. One girl did every problem assigned. The class made an average of 72 per cent. Their work consists of general arithmetic but particularly fractions. The greater part of the questions were on fractions and their applications as far as possible to business matters.

(4) *Geography*.—Class A.—There are five girls and thirteen boys in this class. Their study for the session had been Africa. We gave them as far as time would allow a pretty thorough examination on its physical features, political divisions, colonies and the countries to which they belong, the chief cities, races, products, and chief exports. We found they had obtained through the means of a very fine dissected map which Mr. Wickens had lately designed, a most excellent knowledge of the whole continent, and particularly of South Africa and the localities affected by the present war. Every place of any note in connection with the war had been thoroughly mastered, as to its location, character and direction from other chief points.

(5) *Typewriting*.—Twenty-three pupils of both sexes were observed as they wrote to dictation a short business letter and a bill of goods. The work on the whole is very creditable, the errors were not many and not serious. Their ideas of the proper form to use in a bill and their arrangement of the items were in most cases good. Apart entirely from the mere utilitarian value of this subject to them, it is very evident that it gives a certain feeling of independence. They certainly have learned how to write a very fair letter, and by this means are put, in this respect, on a level with seeing persons. With the addition of the phonograph, perhaps, this subject could be made of greater utility to them.

(*d*) MR. MCLEAN'S CLASSES.

(1) *Arithmetic*.—Class D.—Twenty-seven in class, twelve seniors and fifteen juniors. Limit of former: Simple rules, definitions, easy problems. Of latter: Addition and subtraction, easy problems. The seniors, with one exception, did good work; the juniors not quite so good. The seniors, except the one, all obtained 60 and 100 per cent. They had been well taught; answered readily and accurately.

(2) *Geography*.—Class C.—Seventeen in class. Limit: Canada in detail, map work. The answering of this class was remarkably good. They were examined in detail on Canada, the several provinces, the Dominion and local governments, the constitutional limits of their power, principal rivers, lakes and canals, railroads, etc. The tone of the class was good, the order excellent.

(3) *Object Class*.—Sixteen in class. Limit: Stories about animals, description, sources and uses of coal, chalk, the principal spices, etc. The object was placed, in turn, in the pupil's hand when he or she gave an account of its properties, where found and its uses. The answering was very satisfactory and very prompt.

(4) *Grammar*.—" C."—There are twenty-two boys and girls in this class who had evidently been very well taught the simple elements of grammar. There were in this, as in every class, a few who did not do well; but the class showed that very good teaching had been done. Over half the class answered 50 per cent. of the questions. One lad answered all; four others answered 90 per cent. of them. They speak very correctly, and correct errors in English very well.

(5) *Reading*.—This class is composed of four different grades of pupils, some learning the very small words on a card, and the rest using the 1st, 2nd and 3rd books. There are fifteen in all. Each pupil examined first on reading and secondly upon individual words, to test his ability to recognize these apart from the context. They read with fair expression and can explain the meanings of the words used. Particular attention was given to spelling. A very fair set of words was given to each pupil; four spelt all correctly; four others 95 per cent. of them. The average was nearly 87 per cent.

(6) *Writing*.—B.—The class was given a quotation, a set of figures and a selection of capital letters, with their own names. The writing is fairly legible. The average mark is 54 per cent.

(7) *Bible Class, Boys*.—B.—This is certainly a class it would be difficult to praise too highly. They had learned the books of the Bible, St. Paul's missionary journeys, general apostolic history and many other matters, mastering them thoroughly. In con-

nection with the missionary journeys we used a map and found the pupils were able to follow the course thoroughly. Gave them a thorough examination in spelling, taking proper names of persons and places. Spelling most excellent.

(e) Miss Messmore's Classes.

(1) *Bible and Arithmetic.*—Thirteen in this class were examined. For little ones they had a very fair knowledge of the sacred writings; knew something of the Creation, the flood, the story of Joseph, Samson, David, Solomon, the life and death of the Saviour. Sometimes their ready answering was surprising. One got 100 per cent., two 84 per cent., three 70 per cent. In arithmetic, the limit was addition, subtraction and the multiplication table. Within this limit they did pretty satisfactory work.

(2) *Kindergarten Class.*—The same as above. The usual work was done satisfactorily, and the children seemed to enjoy themselves.

(3) *Cooking Class.*—This class is necessarily small, the room used for the purpose being quite small. While we were present they mixed the ingredients of a cottage pudding, peeled some potatoes and stoned some raisins. They described the plan of cooking a steak in answer to questions by their instructor. They have had quite an extensive course, as will be seen by the programme of work done, of which the following is a part: How to make porridge and gruel; the various ways of boiling meat; how to prepare four kinds of vegetable soup; methods of making layer cake, ginger cookies, boiled and baked custards, etc. The room and the utensils are scrupulously clean and the young cooks are tidy as cooks ought to be.

(f) Mr. Padden's Classes.

(1) *Reading.*—D.—The pupils are quite young, and of course the reading is quite elementary. Several of them are yet in their letters, others are able to read small words A very fair number did well. The teacher has certainly aroused a spirit of enthusiasm among them. The spelling of very nearly all was good. Thirteen pupils in the class.

(g) Miss Haycock's Bible Class.

Seven members. Limit: Early Scripture history; parables and miracles; birth of Christ; the Beatitudes; quotations; part St. John's gospel. A bright class, well taught and prompt and accurate in answering; had covered the whole ground. Average of marks, 87 per cent.

(h) Miss Moore's Bible Class.

Limit: The gospel narratives. Nine in a class. They manifested a very satisfactory acquaintance with the leading facts of our Saviour's life from his birth at Bethlehem to his death on Calvary. The answering, attention and order were creditable to themselves and their excellent teacher.

We must, in conclusion, express our obligations to the Principal and staff for the courtesies extended to us and the help afforded during the examination.

Respectfully submitted.

M. J. KELLY,
WM. WILKINSON, Examiners.

Brantford, July 10th, A.D. 1900.

REPORT OF MUSICAL EXAMINER.

HAMILTON, June 12th, 1900.

To Dr. T. F. CHAMBERLAIN,

Inspector of Public Charities, Toronto, Ont.

SIR.—Having spent two days in the individual examination of the result of the year's work in the music classes of the Ontario Institution for the Blind, I have the honor of reporting :

The teachers are unchanged, Mr. Burt being in charge of the organ and vocal music, with Misses Moore and Crompton as assistants in the piano department ; the theory and musical history classes being in charge of Miss Moore.

The organ students numbered seven, in various grades of study, and their progress was satisfactory, though the class is not as advanced as in some previous years. It has, I believe, been an inconvenience, that the electric wind power has been out of order.

The piano students number 42, and generally do credit to themselves and their teachers. While deficient in freedom of touch, they certainly possess great mechanical correctness, blundering, and mistakes being rare, while in music of involved construction each voice is given its value, with a carefulness and exactness too often lacking in seeing pupils. These characteristics would seem to spring naturally from their methods of learning—dictation by the teacher, writing out in point print by the pupil, and the careful memorizing of each part from the copy thus obtained. The process is slow, but appears very sure, and the work of a session has never shown a better result in this department than the one now closed.

In the theory classes (under the charge of Miss Moore) there were nine pupils who are also students of musical history. They are in various grades, from elementary harmony to four part counterpoints, and the papers submitted were fairly satisfactory, but I think the excitement and hurry of the closing days of the session are not favorable for perfect correctness.

The singing classes have always formed a strong feature in the music of the Institute, and this year is no exception. Embracing about fifty pupils under the management and teaching of Mr. Burt, they sang most effectively several part songs of differing character, with a unanimity of attack, tune and expression, and a clear utterance of the words, rarely heard. There is a want of male voices to maintain a perfect balance of tone, arising partly, I think, from a deficiency of the voices required, but partly from less aptitude and desire for singing on the part of the boys.

The same remark applies to the chapel singing, which, excellent as it is, would be greatly increased in body of sound and emotional value if the boys would take their part with the same spirit as the girls take theirs. They have been urged to do so, but there is still room for much improvement.

The kindergarten is smaller and less vigorous than in previous sessions, but is always pleasant to see and hear.

The tuning class has this year received the advantage to be derived from the appointment of a resident teacher, Mr. Hayter, which has undoubtedly strengthened its value, and the students number 22. It is open to all, but, as in other branches, all are not equally qualified for the work, and some fall by the way, while others achieve success. Several students of past years are now filling good positions in piano factories, and, as blindness offers no hindrance to skilful tuning (a power always in demand), it appears to offer a fairly reliable means of self-support, a matter of practical importance. The work submitted was entirely satisfactory. I have this year for the first time made a point of attending the closing entertainment, which furnished a good illustration of the result of the year's work. It was entirely in the hands of the pupils, even to the tuning of the pianos used, and strongly evidenced the qualities of which I have spoken—accuracy and freedom from all blundering or tangling. In the singing of "God Save the Queen," which closed the musical session, there was no need to urge the efforts of either boys or girls. They sang with a will which might offer them a lesson for other occasions.

Thanking all with whom I have been brought into connection for their courtesy and assistance, I am,

Your obedient servant,

R. S. AMBROSE.

OCULIST'S REPORT OF EXAMINATION OF PUPILS OF INSTITUTION FOR BLIND.

To T. F. CHAMBERLAIN, M.D.,
Inspector.

As per instructions from you, with the kind assistance of the Principal, Mr. Dymond, I made an examination of the pupils of the Ontario Institution for the Blind on April 2nd, 3rd and 4th, there being 130 present at the time, and three temporarily absent, making a total of 74 male and 59 female pupils in attendance. Of this number 12 males and 7 females, 19 in all, were examined for the first time since entering the Institution.

The following table will give a general idea of the condition of vision found:

Class.		Male.	Female.	Total.
1.	Without perception of light in either eye.....	25	10	35
2.	Perception of light only, in one eye..........	8	9	17
3.	" " in both eyes	6	9	15
4.	Limited objective vision in one eye..........	18	11	29
5.	" " " in both eyes	15	19	34
		72	58	130

The standard of admission followed by Mr. Dymond is "such defect of vision as renders education by ordinary means impossible or injurious." Of classes 1, 2 and 3 there is no remark to be made in this respect, but of classes 4 and 5 the question of eligibility arises, which, however, is not difficult to decide, for while there were at least seven males and five females who have vision enough in one eye to do a limited amount of reading, and three males who would be able to read large type from the blackboard, yet it is very evident that to attempt to gain an education at an ordinary school would be for such not only unsuccessful, but in quite a proportion of these cases disastrous to the little vision left to them, which fact is well illustrated in a few of the cases; one in particular, where the opthalmologist, under whose care the case was before entering the Institution, predicted blindness in a short time in the ordinary mode of life, showing that not only is there a wonderful work done here in the way of education by the peculiar methods adapted to the needs of the blind, but also an important one of preservation. On the other hand, two males who recently entered were found to have unquestionably sufficient vision in one eye to enable them to be educated in the ordinary way. They will be retired at the close of the current session.

The diseases causing blindness with the number of cases, and percentage affected by each disease, are :—

	Males.	Females.	Per cent.
Cataract (Congenital and Lamellar)................	12	10	16.92
Ophthalmia Neonatorum	13	9	16.92
Atrophy of Optic Nerve	11	9	15.39
Injury	7	2	6.92
Injury of one eye followed by Sympathetic Ophthalmia in the other	5	3	6.15
Retinitis Pigmentosa..........................	2	5	5.39
Microphthalmos	4	3	5.39
Corneal Ulcers	3	2	3.85
Detached Retina..	4	..	3.09
Scarlet Fever	3	1	3.09
Measles..	1	2	2.30
Interstitial Keratitis	..	2	1.53
Intra-uterine Keratitis	..	2	1.53
Choroiditis	1	1	....
Hydrophthalmos................................	1	1	....
Congenital Defects............................	1	1	....
Refractive Errors	1	1	....
Irido Choroiditis..............................	1	1	....
Trachoma......................................	..	1	.77
Brain Fever....................................	..	1	....
Undetermined	2	1	....
	72	58	....

Cataract (Congenital and Lamellar) (22 cases) and Ophthalmia Neonatorum (22 cases), are equally great offenders, with Atrophy of the Optic Nerve (20 cases) not far behind, these three diseases alone being responsible for almost half the blindness in the Institution. They are pretty equally divided, proportionately, between the males and females.

Among the Cataracts (22 cases) a number have been operated, with the result shown below, which, however, are no argument against operation since naturally only those which were not brilliantly successful are found here.

Twenty-two eyes have been operated on in 15 pupils, one pupil lost one eye with the vision of the other improved; another lost one and would not allow the other to be operated on, while a third lost one eye with doubtful improvement in the other.

	Males.	Females.
Eyes in which vision was improved	6	4
" " doubtfully improved	6	3
" " lost	3	..

The family histories of the children with Cataracts reveal a certain tendency for more than one member of a family to be afflicted with the disease, in as much as one female pupil with cataract (whose parents were cousins), has four brothers similarly affected.

Two other families have respectively two boys and one girl, and one boy and one girl now pupils from the same cause, while the father of one male pupil had Congenital Cataract successfully operated on in childhood. The remaining cases belong one to each family, and range from the first to the sixth child. Nystagmus of varying degree is almost universally present in these cases.

Of Ophthalmia Neonatorum (22 cases), next to the frequency of the disease, the most striking feature is its high percentage, viz., 18.18 per cent., found in illegitimate children, and further, with the exception of one case, the blindness of all the illegitimate children in the Institution is due to Ophthalmia Neonatorum. Including these, which we hope were the first, nine of the cases, or nearly half of them, were the first born, they seeming most liable to the disease. Its effect on the eye is as a rule very disfiguring as may be judged from the following list of conditions in the 44 eyes affected :—

Phthisis Bulbi	16
Anterior Staphyloma	12
Opaque Cornea with Anterior Synechia	7
Opaque Cornea	6
Removed	3
	44

These children mainly belong to a class in humble circumstances, as the avocations of the parents named in the register show. Of the illegitimate children nothing of course if known of the fathers.

Atrophy of the Optic Nerve (20 cases). A cause for the disease is assigned only in a few cases :—

Hereditary Syphilis,	4	cases, affected at ages	8, 7, 8 years and birth.
Brain Tumor,	1	" " "	14 years.
Sunstroke,	1	" " "	5 years.
Meningitis,	1	" " "	1 year.
No cause assigned,	4	" " "	2, 4, 8 and 10 years.
	11		

The rest of the 20 cases of Atrophy, or nearly half were born blind, or with impaired vision. Three of these are brothers; two in another family are sisters, of which five children are similarly affected, while one other had a brother, a former pupil, similarly affected.

Injuries (9 cases). Although the number of injuries not followed by Sympathetic Ophthalmia is one in excess of those in which this unfortunate event did happen, it is of no significance from a statistical standpoint, and does not alter the deplorable fact that sooner or later penetrating injuries of one eye are very likely to be followed by Sympathetic Ophthalmia in the other, because in most of these cases where it did not follow, the uninjured eye was previously useless; or both eyes were injured simultaneously in such accidents as powder and chemical explosions.

The statement that "An eye which has been destroyed in consequence of injury is a constant source of danger to the other eye," is exemplified here. The periods intervening between the injury to the one eye and the Sympathetic Ophthalmia in the other are in the eight cases, one week, one month, three months, one year, six years, and three unknown. In six cases the injury was of a penetrating nature, and the other two being "a blow from a stick" and "a fall," also may have been penetrating. As might be expected the males are considerably in excess in this class.

Retinitis Pigmentosa (7 cases). Consanguinity is known in the parents of five of these.

Cases.	Parents.	Other members similarly affected.
No. 1........	Second cousins..........	....
No. 2........	Mother blind at age of 60.	....
No. 3........	....	....
No. 4........	Second cousins	2 sisters and 3 brothers.
No. 5........	Distant cousins..........	1 sister and 1 cousin.
Nos. 6 and 7..	Cousins. (Nos. 6 and 7 are brothers).	

Scarlet Fever is attributed as the cause of blindness in four cases, one case still retains one normal eye, all the other eyes but one, which was removed, are shrunken. The ages at which they were affected were, respectively, five months, three, four and seven years

Measles in three cases is said to have caused blindness, but in two of them it is questionable, one having Optic Atrophy, the other old Retinitis, while the third, in which the balls are shrunken may have been due to measles.

Congenital Defects constitute only 1.5 per cent. of the total number, but are remarkable. One, a male, has complete absence of the Iris in both eyes, Iridermia. The other a female, has congenital absence of one eye. Monophthalmos, a very rare condition, and a Colobomia of the Iris is the other. The family history of both cases shows no defect.

Of the two cases of Refractive Errors, one has a very high degree of Myopia, his father was also myopic. The other had a bad case of Mixed Astigmatism. Glasses are of but little assistance to either of these pupils.

One female, with one eye shrunken, and an Anterior Staphyloma of the other is said to have been rendered so by brain fever.

The eyes in which the cause of blindness is unknown are mostly in a shrunken condition.

B. C. BELL, M.B.

BRANTFORD, May 18th, 1900.

MAINTENANCE AND EXPENDITURES

For the year ending 30th September, A D. 1900, compared with the preceding year.

Item.	Service.	Year ending 30th Sept., 1899. Average No. of pupils 129.			Year ending 30th Sept., 1900. Average No. of pupils 126.		
		Total expenditure, 1899.	Weekly cost per pupil.	Yearly cost per pupil.	Total expenditure, 1900.	Weekly cost per pupil.	Yearly cost per pupil.
		$ c.	c. m.	$ c.	$ c.	c. m.	$ c.
1	Medicines and medical comforts.	161 36	2 4	1 25	110 44	1 6	88
2	Butchers' meat, fish and fowls..	2,000 00	29 8	15 50	1,876 66	28 2	14 81
3	Flour, bread and biscuits	596 64	8 8	4 62	517 06	7 6	4 10
4	Butter and lard	1,038 81	12 5	8 05	1,082 53	16 5	8 59
5	General groceries	1,430 28	21 3	11 08	1,545 90	23 8	12 42
6	Fruit and vegetables	331 49	4 8	2 53	390 11	5 9	3 09
7	Bedding, clothing and shoes....	623 20	9 2	4 83	419 61	6 4	3 33
8	Fuel, wood, coal and gas	2,655 85	39 5	20 58	2,826 35	41 6	22 43
9	Light—electric and gas	885 20	13 1	6 84	881 92	13 4	6 99
10	Laundry, soap and cleaning	338 31	5.	2 62	376 58	5 4	2 82
11	Furniture and furnishings......	379 54	5 6	2 94	479 53	7 3	3 80
12	Farm and garden, feed and fodder	619 21	9 2	4 80	867 55	13	6 80
13	Repairs and alterations	769 61	11 4	5 96	607 86	9 2	4 82
14	Advertising, printing, stationery and postage	648 32	9 6	5 02	582 64	9	4 62
15	Books, apparatus and appliances	880 60	13 1	6 82	873 04	13 3	6 92
16	Miscellaneous, unenumerated ..	1,379 49	20 5	10 69	1,214 54	18 5	9 64
17	Pupils' sittings at church.......	252 00	3 7	1 95	242 00	3 7	1 92
18	Rent of water hydrants	160 00	2 3	1 24	160 00	2 6	1 35
19	Extra water supply.........	40 67	6	32	59 94	9	47
20	Salaries and wages	17,346 68	261	135 72	17,638 78	269 2	139 99
	Total	32,537 26	485	252 22	32,753 04	498 3	259 15

Average number of pupils in 1899, 129.
" " " 1900, 126.

CPSIA information can be obtained
at www.ICGtesting.com
Printed in the USA
BVHW060243231118
533618BV00023BA/3183/P

9 780260 05182